What Makes Me A
MUSLIM?

Catherine M. Petrini

KIDHAVEN PRESS
A part of Gale, Cengage Learning

GALE
CENGAGE Learning™

Detroit • New York • San Francisco • New Haven, Conn • Waterville, Maine • London

GALE
CENGAGE Learning

Picture credits

Cover photo: © Michael
 Yamashita/CORBIS
AP/Wide World Photos (center), 11
© Archivo Iconografico S.A./
 CORBIS, 5, 14
© Najlah Feanny/SABA/CORBIS, 21
HIP/Scala/Art Resource, NY, 9
© Historical Picture Archive/
 CORBIS, 6
© Zahid Hussein/Reuters/CORBIS, 25
Fayaz Kabli/Reuters/Landov, 37

© Ed Kashi/CORBIS, 18
Mian Khursheed/Reuters/
 Landov, 15
Erich Lessing/Art Resource, NY, 29
Brandy Noon, 11
PhotoDisc, 32–33 (all photos)
© Reuters/CORBIS (bottom), 11© Steve
 Raymer/CORBIS, 22
© Reuters/CORBIS, 17, 31, 34, 39
© Kurt Stier/CORBIS (top), 11
Suhaib Salem/Reuters/Landov,
 26

© 2005 Gale, Cengage Learning

For more information, contact
KidHaven Press
27500 Drake Rd.
Farmington Hills, MI 48331-3535
Or you can visit our Internet site at gale.cengage.com

LIBRARY OF CONGRESS CATALOGING-IN-PUBLICATION DATA

Petrini, Catherine M.
  Muslim / by Catherine M. Petrini.
   p. cm. — (What makes me a—?
  Includes bibliographical references and index.
   Summary: Discusses the beginnings of Islam, what Muslims believe, how they practice their faith, their religious holidays, and the challenges facing their religion.
   ISBN 0-7377-2265-7 (hardcover : alk. paper)
   1. Islam—Juvenile literature. 2. Muslims—Juvenile literature. I. Title. II. Series.

  BP161.3.P47 2005
  297—dc22

                                                2004014526

Printed in the United States of America
 3 4 5 6 7 12 11 10 09 08

CONTENTS

CHAPTER ONE

How Did My Religion Begin?

Fourteen hundred years ago, an angel visited a man named Muhammad. The angel, Gabriel, appeared to him many times. He told Muhammad that God, or Allah, was unhappy with the way people were living their lives and practicing religion. He gave Muhammad instructions for teaching people a different way.

In Muhammad's town of Mecca, in what is now Saudi Arabia, most people worshipped many gods. The angel told him there was only one God and that worshipping anyone or anything other than Allah was the worst possible sin. The angel also said people should submit to Allah's will. In other words, they should do what Allah wanted them to do. That is why the religion Muhammad taught is called Islam, which means "submission." The angel also said people should struggle against their own selfishness. He said God wanted everyone to take responsibility for helping those in need and for creating a fair and peaceful society.

Muhammad spent the rest of his life teaching people about God's plan. His words inspired people and gained him many followers. Eventually some of his followers copied the messages from God into a book called the

As two armies prepare to battle, the angel Gabriel gives Muhammad the Koran, the holy book of Islam. Out of respect for Muhammad, this illustration hides his face.

Koran. Today the Koran still forms the core of Islamic beliefs.

A Nomadic Childhood

Muhammad was born in A.D. 570, about forty years before the angel's first visit. He belonged to the Quraysh, the most important and powerful tribe in Mecca. His father died before Muhammad was born. His mother died when he was young. Growing up as an orphan caused

The Kabah temple sits in the center of Mecca, depicted here as it appeared in Muhammad's time. The Kabah remains the holiest house of worship in all Islam.

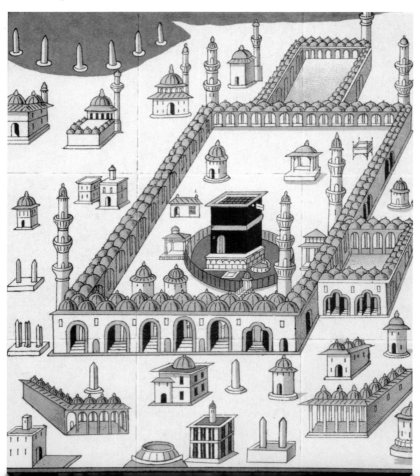

Muhammad to care about the least powerful in his society: women, children, poor people, and slaves.

Muhammad spent his early childhood with a family of **nomads** in the desert. Eventually he was sent back to Mecca, where he lived first with his grandfather and then with his uncle.

"The Trustworthy One"

Muhammad's uncle traded goods. Mecca was a good place for traders, because it bustled with travelers from foreign lands. People came to visit a temple called the Kabah. This was—and is—the most important house of worship in the Muslim world. The best-known part of the Kabah is a large black stone in the wall of the building. The stone is a meteorite, a chunk of rock that fell from space. Because it came from the heavens, **pagan** worshippers called it a sign from the gods. Christian, Jewish, and Muslim pilgrims also respect the black stone. They believe it was one of the stones used by Adam, the first man, to build the original temple. Later, the **prophet** Abraham—ancestor of Jews, Christians, and Muslims—set the same stone into the wall when he rebuilt the Kabah. In Muhammad's day, the Kabah was visited mostly by pagan worshippers. Statues and pictures of pagan gods filled the temple and the area around it.

Many people who visited the Kabah brought goods to trade with local merchants such as Muhammad's uncle. His uncle also traveled to distant places to trade with people in other lands. Such trips were made on caravans, long lines of camels that carried products and people across the desert. Working on his uncle's caravans, Muhammad learned to make fair trades and to talk with all kinds of people. By his teens, he was known for honesty among traders. His nickname was "al-Amin," or "the Trustworthy One."

A Rich, Beautiful, and Noble Lady

At the age of twenty-five, Muhammad led a caravan carrying goods to Syria, a Middle Eastern country about 800 miles (1,287km) north of Mecca. The goods belonged to a wealthy widow named Khadijah. With Muhammad in charge, Khadijah made more money than ever before. Afterward, one of her servants raved to her about Muhammad. He praised the young man's skill and fairness in business and his friendship and good sense on the journey.

Khadijah sent a friend to ask Muhammad if he would consider marrying a rich, beautiful, and noble lady. The marriage was arranged, even though she was forty years old—fifteen years older than he was.

Muhammad and Khadijah were happy together. They had four healthy daughters. Fifteen years after their wedding, Muhammad journeyed alone to a mountaintop cave near Mecca. He returned awestruck with the story of the angel's first **revelations**. Khadijah understood the importance of his story even before he did. She realized Allah had chosen her husband to be a prophet. Muhammad himself was unsure. He returned to the mountaintop, and the angel Gabriel appeared to him again. Muhammad, frightened, hurried home.

The angel Gabriel is often shown with a trumpet, a symbol of his important message. He appeared to Muhammad many times.

Again his wife comforted him and encouraged him to believe the angel's words. Finally Muhammad accepted his mission and began spreading Allah's revelations.

Forced Out of Mecca

With Khadijah's help, Muhammad attracted some followers in the years after his first revelation in 610. But most Meccans did not believe his claim that there was only one god. Mecca's wealth depended on the popularity of the Kabah as a temple filled with pagan **idols**. If travelers rejected their pagan gods and turned their backs on idol worship, they might stop coming to Mecca. If that happened, residents would lose their major source of wealth and prestige.

Muhammad's tribe, the Quraysh, had the most to lose. As the keepers of the Kabah, they profited the most from it. To protect their position, leaders of the Quraysh urged Muhammad to put an end to his teachings. They even offered to make him head of the tribe if he would stop spreading his faith. Muhammad refused, saying, "I would not do so—even if you placed the sun in my right hand and the moon in my left hand."[1]

When it became clear that Muhammad would not change his mind, his critics turned violent. Some of his followers were beaten or tortured. Some fled to Abyssinia (now Ethiopia, in northern Africa), where they were sheltered by Christians. After threats against his life, Muhammad finally slipped away from Mecca in the night. He fled to the city of Yathrib (now called Medina, in Saudi Arabia), where he lived for the rest of his life.

The Cradle of Islam

Medina

Persecuted for his beliefs, Muhammad fled to Medina in A.D. 622.

Mecca

Persian Gulf

S a u d i   A r a b i a

Red Sea

Mecca's Kabah temple is the most important place of worship in the Muslim world.

The annual pilgrimage to Mecca brings together Muslims from all over the world.

Europe

Asia

Africa

Spreading the Faith

Muhammad's flight to Medina is known as the Hejira, which means "departure." The year of the Hejira, 622, is the beginning of the Muslim calendar. It marks the founding of the first Muslim state. In Medina, pagans welcomed Muhammad's message and accepted him as their leader. They quickly converted to Islam and began teaching others about the religion. Muhammad also became friendly with the Jewish and Christian tribes there. He told Muslims to treat them with respect. His vision for a Muslim state, based on the angel's revelations, was of a place where all who worshipped one God could live together peacefully.

Relations between Medina and pagan Mecca were less peaceful. For eight years Meccan soldiers fought against Muhammad's smaller, poorly armed forces. Finally, in 630, Muhammad took control of Mecca. Once there, he banned the worship of idols and reclaimed the Kabah for the followers of Allah.

By this time, Islam was spreading rapidly throughout the Middle East. For centuries the region had been torn by wars among **Arab** tribes. Muhammad taught them that their common faith was more important than tribal disputes. Under Muhammad's rule, the tribes became united by their new religion. After Muhammad's death in 632, Islam continued to spread with great speed. The peace and social reform that Muhammad had set in motion were already changing the world.

CHAPTER TWO

What Do
I Believe?

Muslims all over the world share the same basic beliefs. The most important is the belief in one God, or Allah. In fact, Muslims believe so strongly in worshipping none other but the true God that they consider it sinful even to make idols, because people might worship them instead. Muslims respect Muhammad as Allah's messenger, but they do not worship him or consider him divine. They believe he was the last of a series of prophets. Another messenger they respect is Jesus. They believe that Jesus, like Muhammad, was a prophet but not a god.

Muslims look to an earlier prophet, Abraham, as the father of their faith. Abraham, who lived four thousand years ago, is also the father of Judaism and Christianity. The Bible and the Koran both tell his story. He submitted to God's will and in return was able to father children in his old age. One of these children was Ishmael,

In this painting, the patriarch Abraham walks with his sons Isaac and Ishmael. Muslims believe they are descendants of Ishmael.

whom Muslims claim as their ancestor. Muslims consider their religion to be a revival of Abraham's faith. They believe the angel's revelations were Allah's way of restoring its pure form.

The Key to Islam

The key to Islamic beliefs is the Koran, which Muslims believe is Allah's message to humanity. The Koran is a book of 114 chapters called suras. Within the suras are descriptions of how God wants people to live and worship. The Koran contains many kinds of information, including poetry and prose, prayers, warnings, instructions, and history lessons. Much of it explores three themes: God's supreme power; that people must be responsible for their own actions; and the certainty of an afterlife.

Muslim students study the Koran at a school in Pakistan. Muslims believe the Koran is the true word of God.

The Muslim concept of an afterlife begins with the Day of Judgment. No one but Allah knows when that day will come. Muslims believe that on that day, all human beings who ever lived will answer for everything they have said or done. People who did good deeds and submitted to God will be admitted to paradise, a garden of complete happiness. The others will be sentenced to hell. One of the main purposes of the Koran is to help Muslims bow to Allah's will and live as he commands, so they can enter paradise.

Muslims believe that all people, no matter what race or religion they were born to, can choose to submit themselves to Allah's will and earn his favor. In Muhammad's final speech to his followers, he said, "There is no superiority for an Arab over a non-Arab nor for a non-Arab over an Arab, neither for a white man over a black man nor a black man over a white man except the superiority gained through consciousness of God. Indeed the noblest among you is the one who is most deeply conscious of God."[2]

The Word of God

Muslims believe that the Koran was not written by Muhammad but was told to him by Allah, through the angel Gabriel. They consider it the actual word of God. Because it was given to Muhammad in Arabic, Muslims believe it should be read only in Arabic. They also believe it is important to recite the Koran aloud, because that is how Muhammad received the revelations and taught them to people. The angel's first words to

Muslim women recite from the Koran. Many Muslims memorize the entire Koran and teach it to others.

him told him to tell others what was going to be revealed to him, so that everyone could hear and understand God's wishes. Many Muslims memorize the entire book so they can pass it on to others.

Like most people of his time, Muhammad could not read or write. But Muslims consider themselves (along with Jews and Christians) to be "People of the Book," followers of the written word of God. The Koran urges Muslims to become educated so they can read and understand God's message. Many Muslims also learn calligraphy (a decorative style of writing), so they can glorify Allah by using Arabic words and verses from the Koran as beautiful decorations in art and architecture.

Two Types of Muslims

While all Muslims accept the Koran as the word of God, they do disagree about some things. The two largest groups within Islam are Sunni Muslims and Shia Muslims.

The split between the two groups began after Muhammad's death. Muhammad died without choosing a **caliph**, a person to lead the religion after him. Some of his followers wanted the position to go to Muhammad's son-in-law, Ali, who was also his cousin. They believed God chose Muhammad's family to lead Islam. They were outnumbered by those who wanted to select the best-qualified person through a vote. Eventually, Ali did become the fourth caliph. His supporters, the Shia, thought

Shia Muslim students attend a school in Lebanon. Shia believe that only the descendants of Muhammad should rule Islam.

Ali should have been the first caliph and that his descendants should continue to rule Islam.

Those who wanted to choose their caliphs by a vote became the Sunnis. Today nearly 85 percent of Muslims worldwide are Sunnis. They respect their religious leaders, or **imams**, as teachers and protectors of the faith. However, they consider them to be men like other men, without any special charge from God.

Although in the minority worldwide, Shias are the majority in some places, most notably in Iran and Iraq. Their religious community can be led only by a relative of Muhammad. Because Shias believe their imams have been chosen by God, they consider them sinless, with final authority to interpret God's will. Shias follow their imams not only in religious matters, but in political ones as well.

Despite Sunnis' and Shias' different attitudes toward their leaders and their history, they agree on the most important parts of their faith: a belief in Allah as the one true God, an acceptance of the Koran as the word of God, and a devotion to the basic practices and principles of Islam.

CHAPTER THREE

How Do I Practice My Faith?

For all Muslims, the practice of Islam follows instructions given in the Koran as well as other teachings of Muhammad. The most basic practices are five activities known as the *arkan*, or the Five Pillars of Islam. These five observances, listed in the Koran, are simple. But making them a way of life requires dedication and self-discipline.

Faith, Prayer, and Charity

The first pillar of Islam is *shahadah*, the declaration of faith. This simple, one-sentence declaration states that there is no god except Allah and that Muhammad is his messenger. To become a Muslim, all a person must do is state the *shahadah* in front of witnesses. After that, the *shahadah* is repeated as part of a Muslim's regular prayers.

The second pillar is *salah*, or prayer. A Muslim prays five times a day, following a certain sequence of steps. All over the world, Muslims pray at daybreak, noon, midafternoon, sunset, and evening. At those times, all men and women—and older boys and girls—are supposed to stop whatever they are doing. They perform a ritual washing, and then they turn to face Mecca and worship Allah.

The prayers are made up of certain passages from the Koran, praises of Allah, and the *shahadah*. As worshippers pray, they perform a series of movements:

Muslim Americans pray during one of the five times Muslims must pray each day. Prayer is one of the Five Pillars of Islam.

standing, bowing, kneeling, touching the ground with their foreheads, and sitting. They always end with another recitation of the *shahadah,* and then say the "peace greeting" twice: "Peace be upon all of you and the mercy and blessing of God."

Muslims prefer to worship together. This shows their unity in Allah. On Fridays, Muslim men are required to say the noontime prayers together in a **mosque**, where an imam leads the prayers and gives a sermon. Most of the time, however, daily prayers can be said either alone or in groups. Muslims may pray at a mosque or wherever they happen to be. Many Muslims carry a small prayer rug so they will always have a clean place to pray.

Muslim men touch their heads to the floor as they pray in a mosque. Muslims often worship together.

The third pillar is the *zakat,* a requirement that all Muslims follow God's will by helping the poor. Every year Muslims must give at least 2.5 percent of their wealth to people in the community who are less fortunate than they are. In addition, they donate money for projects such as the construction and upkeep of hospitals, religious schools, and mosques.

The Fast of Ramadan

The fourth pillar of Islam is the yearly **fast** of Ramadan. Ramadan, the ninth month of the Islamic calendar, is when Muhammad received his first revelation from Allah. For the entire month, most Muslims fast, or do not eat or drink anything, between dawn and sunset each day. Fasting reminds people to focus on God instead of their physical needs. It also helps them imagine how it feels to be poor and hungry so that they will treat poor people kindly and be thankful for their own blessings. Pregnant women, small children, and sick people are not supposed to fast.

Just before sunrise on the first day of Ramadan, after an early breakfast, it is traditional to open the fast by eating one date. Dates are special to Muslims because Muhammad ate this fruit during his spiritual retreats. Muslims break the Ramadan fast after sunset with a light snack—sometimes just a few dates—with water. Later, families and friends share a simple meal. Many people follow the meal with a trip to the mosque for the regular evening prayer and special Ramadan prayers. Some Muslims recite the entire Koran during

Ramadan, one-thirtieth of the book each night of the month.

Pilgrimage to Mecca

The fifth pillar of Islam is the hajj, or **pilgrimage** to Mecca. Traditionally, every Muslim is supposed to make this pilgrimage to Muhammad's hometown at least once, except for those who are too sick or too poor. The pilgrimage takes place in the last month of the Islamic calendar.

Each year, about 2 million people make the hajj, which is one of the most important events in a Muslim's life. It is not easy to do. Muslims give up time, money, and comfort to undertake what can be a long, difficult journey. Once they arrive in the holy land, they follow a series of prayers and rituals over several days.

When pilgrims approach the area around Mecca, they stop to wash themselves. They want to enter Mecca in a state of purity. They wear special clothes to stand for purity, unity, and equality. Women and girls wear long dresses with scarves over their heads. Men and boys wear two seamless pieces of white cloth, one wrapped around the waist and the other around the upper body. As they dress, pilgrims state aloud their intention of making a pilgrimage: "Here I am, O God, at thy service!"

After entering Mecca, pilgrims go first to the Kabah, the cube-shaped structure known as the House of God. Pilgrims must walk around the Kabah counterclockwise seven times to symbolize their entry into Allah's presence.

A fruit vendor sells dates during Ramadan. Traditionally, Muslims start and break the Ramadan fast with dates.

Pilgrims pray at the Grand Mosque in Mecca during the hajj. Muslims try to make the trip to Mecca at least once in their lifetime.

Throughout the hajj, they pray together and perform other rituals, many of them based on events from Abraham's time.

The hajj is a way for Muslims to worship Allah and remember their history. It also brings people of different races and backgrounds together for prayer, spiritual discussions, and an exchange of ideas.

Rules About Food and Drink

The five pillars are not the only practices shared by Muslims. Islamic law sets out other rules, too. Some deal with food and drink. For example, there are certain rituals for slaughtering animals and readying the meat for eating. Meat that has been prepared correctly is called **halal** and is the only kind that Muslims are supposed to eat. They never eat pork, no matter how the pig is slaughtered. Alcohol is also forbidden, except when needed as medicine.

With believers spread out around the world and coming from many different cultures, Muslims feel it is especially important to follow common practices. The five pillars and other practices of Islam bind them as part of the *ummah,* the worldwide Islamic community.

CHAPTER FOUR

What Holidays Do I Celebrate?

Throughout the world, Muslims follow the Islamic calendar for religious observances. This calendar consists of twelve months. Each month begins with the new Moon. Because it is based on the Moon's cycles rather than the Earth's orbit around the Sun, it is eleven days shorter than the 365-day calendar. This means that the months—and the holidays that take place during them—are not tied to seasons of the year. There are no fixed winter, spring, summer, or fall festivals. Instead Muslims celebrate a variety of festivals that recall their history and help bring them closer to each other and to God.

Feast of the Sacrifice

The most important Muslim holiday is Id al-Adha, the Feast of the Sacrifice. This holiday reminds Muslims of a key event in the life of Abraham. Abraham wanted children all his life but did not have them until he was much older. Then God appeared to him in a dream and asked him to show obedience by killing his son as a sacrifice to God. Abraham loved his son, but he knew he must submit to God's will, so he prepared to kill him. At the last minute, an angel stopped him, saying his willingness was

In this painting, an angel stops Abraham from sacrificing his son to God. The Muslim holiday Id al-Adha celebrates this event.

enough. He had proven his obedience. His son was saved, and Abraham sacrificed a ram instead.

The celebration of that event takes place near the end of the annual pilgrimage and lasts for several days. Muslims take time off from work and school. They pray together and listen to a sermon about Abraham's sacrifice. Then they sacrifice an animal to Allah and have a large feast. Many people exchange gifts.

Holidays Around Ramadan

The holy month of Ramadan is tied to three special holidays. Laylat ul-Barat, the Night of Forgiveness, takes place the month before and is considered the "gateway to Ramadan." Muslims believe that on this night, Allah decides what will happen to each person during the coming year. What happens depends on everyone's actions in the past year. People stay up all night, praying to Allah, asking forgiveness, and giving thanks.

Laylat ul-Qadr, or the Night of Power, takes place toward the end of Ramadan. This is the anniversary of the angel Gabriel's first revelation to Muhammad. In Muslim countries, people celebrate by decorating their towns with strings of lights. They spend the night visiting many different mosques with family and friends, where they pray together in happiness and peace.

When Ramadan ends, Muslims celebrate Id al-Fitr, the Feast of the Breaking of the Fast. This three-day holiday begins when the new Moon appears, marking the end of the month of Ramadan. The Breaking of the Fast is a major event throughout Islam, second only to the

Muslim women pray together to mark the end of the monthlong fast of Ramadan. After finishing their prayers, they will celebrate with family and friends.

Feast of the Sacrifice. People dress in new, colorful clothes. They worship together at mosques, visit family and friends, and exchange gifts and cards. And of course they break their Ramadan fast with festive meals of special foods, including sticky, colorful sweets made of pistachios, milk, and almonds. Somewhere on the table there is usually a plate of dates, in memory of Muhammad.

The Night Journey

Another holy festival is Laylat ul-Isra wal Miraj, or the Night of the Journey and Ascension. This holiday is spent in prayer and reflection, as Muslims recall an important event in Muhammad's spiritual life.

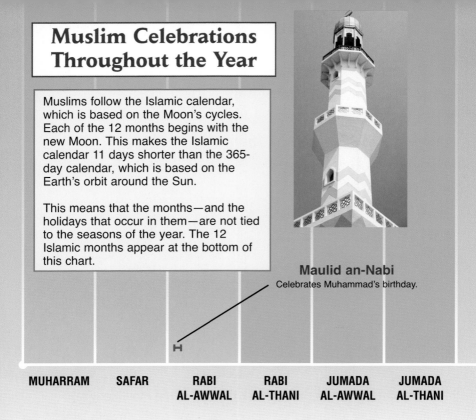

Muslim Celebrations Throughout the Year

Muslims follow the Islamic calendar, which is based on the Moon's cycles. Each of the 12 months begins with the new Moon. This makes the Islamic calendar 11 days shorter than the 365-day calendar, which is based on the Earth's orbit around the Sun.

This means that the months—and the holidays that occur in them—are not tied to the seasons of the year. The 12 Islamic months appear at the bottom of this chart.

Maulid an-Nabi
Celebrates Muhammad's birthday.

H

| MUHARRAM | SAFAR | RABI AL-AWWAL | RABI AL-THANI | JUMADA AL-AWWAL | JUMADA AL-THANI |

Ten years after the first revelation, Muhammad lay sleeping in Mecca. The angel Gabriel woke him, helped him mount a white, winged horse, and guided him on a journey that took place all in one night. First they traveled to Jerusalem, nearly 800 miles (1,287km) away. There, Muhammad prayed with other prophets, including Jesus, Moses, and Abraham.

Then Muhammad was flown up to heaven, where Allah gave him instructions for praying. Originally, Allah said Muslims must pray fifty times a day. On his way back down, Muhammad saw Moses. Moses told him fifty was too many, that humans were too weak to pray that much. Muhammad returned to Allah and asked him to reduce the number. Allah subtracted ten prayers per day. Muhammad traveled back and forth until Allah reduced the

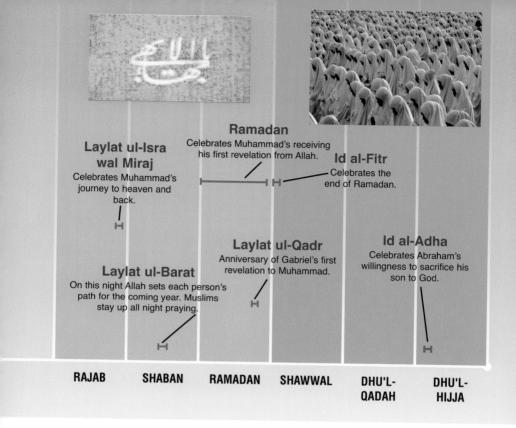

Laylat ul-Isra wal Miraj
Celebrates Muhammad's journey to heaven and back.

Ramadan
Celebrates Muhammad's receiving his first revelation from Allah.

Id al-Fitr
Celebrates the end of Ramadan.

Laylat ul-Barat
On this night Allah sets each person's path for the coming year. Muslims stay up all night praying.

Laylat ul-Qadr
Anniversary of Gabriel's first revelation to Muhammad.

Id al-Adha
Celebrates Abraham's willingness to sacrifice his son to God.

RAJAB	SHABAN	RAMADAN	SHAWWAL	DHU'L-QADAH	DHU'L-HIJJA

prayers to five times per day and Moses was satisfied. Because of Muhammad's bargaining, Muslims believe that those who pray faithfully five times a day will be rewarded as if they had prayed fifty times.

Muslims celebrate the holiday by saying extra prayers and reading the story of the Night of the Journey and Ascension.

Other Holy Days

Muslims observe other holidays, as well. For example, the birthday of Muhammad, Maulid an-Nabi, is a time for celebrating the prophet's life. Many Muslim organizations hold community dinners for the occasion.

Because Muslims come from many cultures and live all over the world, some other holidays are celebrated

Muslims in Indonesia celebrate Muhammad's birthday. Holy days help Muslims feel that they belong to a larger community.

only in some countries or by certain groups of Muslims. All the holy days help Muslims feel that they are part of a community, either local or worldwide. That sense of connection to Islam is more important today than ever before. After all, many Muslims live among people who do not share their faith or understand it.

CHAPTER FIVE

What Challenges Does My Religion Face?

Islam is the fastest-growing religion, with 1.2 billion Muslims in countries around the world. The largest Muslim communities are in Indonesia, Pakistan, Bangladesh, and India. Other Muslims live in the Middle East, where Muhammad lived. Muslims also live in Europe, Asia, the United States, and North Africa.

Throughout the world, Muslims examine and study their faith. Their lives are very different from the lives of people in Muhammad's time. This can make it more difficult to follow some of the rules in the Koran. It is especially hard in countries where Muslims are a minority. For example, praying toward Mecca five times a day is difficult in non-Muslim schools or workplaces, where no place and time are set aside for prayer. Most Muslims do the best they can: They stop their activities as close to the times as possible and pray wherever they can find a quiet spot.

In many communities Muslims cannot follow some of their dietary practices, because there are no Muslim butcher shops that sell halal meat. Many settle for shopping at Jewish butcher shops that sell **kosher** meat. While kosher meat is not halal, it is as close as some Muslims can find in their towns. The slaughtering methods are the same. But halal slaughter must be performed by a Muslim. And there are some differences in the words that are spoken as the animal is killed.

Veiled Women

Even something as simple as choosing what to wear can be a challenge for modern Muslims, especially Muslim women. The Koran requires men and women to dress

Religious Populations of the World

Religion	Population
Islam (Muslims)	1,226,403,000
Catholicism (Catholics)	1,076,951,000
Hinduism (Hindus)	828,130,000
Buddhism (Buddhists)	364,014,000
Protestantism (Protestants)	349,792,000
Judaism (Jews)	14,535,000

| 300 million | 600 million | 900 million | 1.2 billion |

These Muslim women cover their faces in public. In some countries, women who break this rule are severely punished.

modestly. However, it does not define exactly what that means. The lack of clear rules about clothing means that Muslims—or their families or communities—must determine what "modest" clothing is. Different Muslims understand this rule in different ways. Some women drape themselves in yards of concealing fabric. Others wear modern, Western-style clothing. Either choice—or anything in between—can create challenges.

In some non-Muslim countries, women who wear long dresses to cover their bodies or veils to hide their faces or hair may face discrimination because they dress differently from most people. They may not be allowed to wear their veils in certain places, such as schools or some workplaces.

Other Muslim women have no choice but to hide their faces and bodies. This is because a few Muslim countries require women to cover themselves completely when they are in public. Women who break these laws can be severely punished or even killed. Such laws are made by their nation's governments, not by Islam.

Islam and Violence

The worst stereotype faced by Muslims in non-Muslim communities is that Muslims are violent. Islam is often mentioned in news stories about violence in places such as Israel, Afghanistan, Iraq, and Chechnya. Many non-Muslims know little about Islam except for what they see on the news. Hearing so much about Muslims and violence makes them think that Islam is only connected to wars and terrorism. As a result, many Muslims face discrimination and hostility from non-Muslims who are afraid or angry.

One challenge for Muslims is to teach non-Muslims about Islam. At the root of the misunderstanding is jihad, sometimes called the sixth pillar of Islam. *Jihad* means, simply, "a struggle." Many non-Muslims think the term refers only to a holy war—violence by Muslims against nonbelievers. But jihad also has another meaning. After a battle against his enemies, Muhammad once said, "We return from the lesser jihad [struggle] to the greater jihad."[3] He meant that a Muslim's really difficult battle was not a violent struggle against those who threaten the faith, but an internal struggle to overcome personal selfishness, laziness, and greed in order to submit to God's will.

Sometimes, jihad does refer to warfare. The Koran teaches that violence may be necessary to defend the faith. Some Muslims disagree about when violence is necessary. A small number of Muslims believe it is acceptable to kill non-Muslims, because they think their own religion is threatened by other faiths with different values. Sometimes, such Muslims have attacked non-Muslims and claimed they were protecting Islam.

Muslims in New York march to show their support for America's war against terrorism.

Most Muslims are against such violence and work to teach non-Muslims the truth about Islam's jihad. In fact, the Koran allows warfare only when Muslims are under direct attack or are trying to rescue weaker people who are being harmed or oppressed. It prohibits Muslims from harming women and children. And it condemns those who start violence, saying: "Fight in the way of Allah against those who fight against you, but begin not hostilities. Lo! Allah loveth not aggressors."[4]

Overcoming Challenges

To continue practicing their faith while correcting misperceptions about it, Muslims try to teach people about their religion. Islam is a peaceful religion that embraces all who submit themselves to God. Their ideal is a community similar to Muhammad's city of Medina—a place of tolerance and compassion where people of different faiths live side by side in peace.

NOTES

Chapter One: How Did My Religion Begin?

1. Akbar S. Ahmed, *Islam Today: A Short Introduction to the Muslim World.* London: I.B. Tauris, 2002, p. 17.

Chapter Two: What Do I Believe?

2. Ahmed, *Islam Today,* p. 21.

Chapter Five: What Challenges Does My Religion Face?

3. John L. Esposito. *What Everyone Needs to Know About Islam.* New York: Oxford University Press, 2002, p. 117.

4. *The Glorious Qur'an.* Trans. Mohammed Marmaduke Pickthall. Elmhurst, NY: Tahrike Tarsile Qur'an, 2000, p. 41, sura 2:190.

GLOSSARY

Arab: Having to do with a group of people whose culture started on the Arabian peninsula and whose native language is Arabic.

caliph: A person who ruled the Islamic Empire after Muhammad's death. In modern times, with Muslims scattered all over the world, there is no caliph.

fast: An extended time during which a person chooses not to eat, often as part of a religious ritual.

idols: Pictures, statues, or other objects that represent a god and may be worshipped as if they were a god.

halal: Acceptable to eat, under Muslim dietary laws. Halal meat must be ritually slaughtered according to strict rules.

imams: In Sunni Islam, respected men who run a mosque or lead Muslims in prayers; in Shia Islam, descendants of Muhammad are considered to be the rightful leaders of the faith. Shia often capitalize the term.

Islam: The religion practiced by Muslims, which is based on the teachings of Muhammad.

kosher: Acceptable to eat, according to Jewish dietary rules.

mosque: A Muslim place of worship.

nomads: People who have no fixed home but travel from place to place, usually with the seasons.

pagan: A person who worships many gods.

pilgrimage: A journey to a holy place for religious reasons.

prophet: A person who receives and delivers a message from God.

revelations: Important pieces of information given to somebody. In religion, revelations are almost always delivered by God or one of God's messengers.

FOR FURTHER EXPLORATION

Books

Jessica Chalfonte, *I Am Muslim.* New York: Rosen, 1996. This brief, simple introduction describes the basics of Islam through the eyes of a Muslim boy living in Detroit. It includes a glossary.

John Child, *The Rise of Islam.* New York: Bedrick, 1995. A clearly written history of Islam, colorfully illustrated with maps, photographs of Muslim sites, and reproductions of ancient texts and artwork.

Charles Clark, *Islam.* San Diego: Lucent, 2002. This entry in the Religions of the World series covers the history, beliefs, and politics of Islam. Detailed and comprehensive, it includes a glossary, a bibliography, and an index.

John L. Esposito, *What Everyone Needs to Know About Islam.* New York: Oxford University Press, 2002. This book is not written specifically for children, but its logical organization and crystal-clear descriptions make it a valuable overview for any reader who wants to know more about the Muslim world. Focusing on the modern practice of Islam, it uses easy-to-understand language to clear up common misconceptions.

Shahrukh Husain, *What Do We Know About Islam?* New York: Bedrick, 1995. Each chapter of this concise, illustrated introduction asks and answers a single question such as "What is the Muslim holy book?" or "Why is Mecca important?" It also features a colorful time line of events in Muslim history.

Khadijah Knight, *Celebrate Islamic Festivals.* Crystal Lake, IL: Heinemann, 1997. A short introduction to the major Muslim holidays that also contains an excellent glossary.

Philip Wilkinson, *Islam.* New York: Dorling Kindersley, 2002. This richly illustrated guide includes very brief descriptions of a wide variety of aspects of Muslim history and culture. Sections devoted to different countries and regions provide insight into the lives of Muslims worldwide.

Video/DVD

Robert Gardner, *Islam: Empire of Faith.* Gardner Films, 2000. The three-hour PBS series, narrated by actor Ben Kingsley, presents the history of Islam through interviews with experts, historic reenactments, and gorgeous footage of Muslim sites and rituals.

Web Sites

Al-Islam (www.al-islam.com). This one-stop resource for information on the practice of Islam includes verses from the Koran, explanations of Islamic law, and a dictionary of relevant terms.

Islam: Empire of Faith (www.pbs.org/empires/islam). The companion site to PBS's three-hour documentary recounts the first one thousand years of Islam. It also boasts special features such as an interactive time line, profiles of key figures, and lesson plans for teachers.

IslamiCity (www.islamicity.com). Subtitled "Islam and the Global Muslim eCommunity," this site provides a place where Muslims and others with an interest in Islam can learn more and interact with each other. Articles cover a wide variety of topics, including current events, the life of Muhammad, and religious practices.

INDEX